PASTA

Anne Adeney

CW00855004

Contents

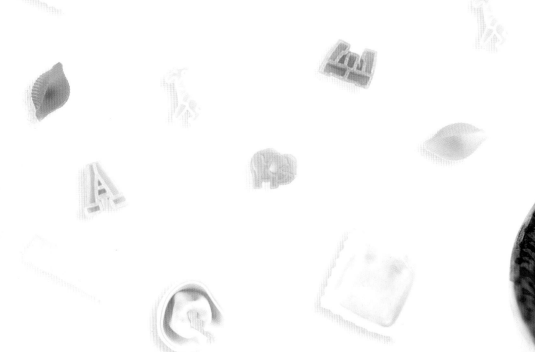

What Is Pasta?

Pasta is a food.
It was first made in Italy.
Now pasta is made all over the world.

Pasta is made from flour and water.
First the flour is mixed with the water.
This makes the pasta dough.

Other foods can be mixed with the dough.
Eggs make the pasta turn yellow.
Spinach makes the pasta turn green.
Tomatoes make the pasta turn red.

Most pasta is hard before it's cooked.
Some pasta is soft before it's cooked.
This pasta is called fresh pasta.
All pasta is soft after it's cooked.

Pasta Shapes

Pasta comes in lots of different shapes.
Some pasta can be long and flat.
Some pasta can be short and round.
Some pasta even looks like animals!

Each pasta shape has a name.
Names for pasta shapes come from Italy.
Long strings of pasta are called spaghetti.
The name spaghetti means string.

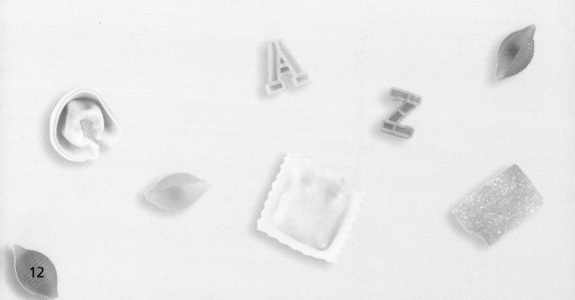

Pasta Dishes

People eat lots of different pasta dishes.
Some people like spaghetti with tomatoes.
Spaghetti is messy to eat!

Which pasta dish do you like?

Index